eam Spirit®

THE NEW YORK JETS

BY

MARK STEWART

Content Consultant
Jason Aikens

NORWOODHOUSE PRESS

CHICAGO, ILLINOIS

Norwood House Press
P.O. Box 316598
Chicago, Illinois 60631

For information regarding Norwood House Press, please visit our website at:
www.norwoodhousepress.com or call 866-565-2900.

PHOTO CREDITS:
All photos courtesy Getty Images except the following:
Associated Press (18, 30, 31), Author's Collection (6, 34 left),
Topps, Inc. (7, 16, 27, 34 right, 37, 40 all, 41 top & bottom right, 43),
Black Book Partners (9, 21, 22, 28, 35 top left & right, 36, 38, 39, 41 left),
Icon SMI (15), TCMA, Ltd. (14, 20), Matt Richman (48).
Cover Photo: Thomas E. Witte/Getty Images
Special thanks to Topps, Inc.

Editor: Mike Kennedy
Designer: Ron Jaffe
Project Management: Black Book Partners, LLC.
Research: Joshua Zaffos
Special thanks to Evan Frankel

LIBRARY OF CONGRESS CATALOGING-IN-PUBLICATION DATA

Stewart, Mark, 1960-
    The New York Jets / by Mark Stewart ; content consultant, Jason Aikens.
        p. cm. -- (Team spirit)
    Includes bibliographical references and index.
    Summary: "Presents the history and accomplishments of the New York Jets
football team. Includes highlights of players, coaches, and awards, quotes,
timelines, maps, glossary and websites"--Provided by publisher.
    ISBN-13: 978-1-59953-330-8 (library edition : alk. paper)
    ISBN-10: 1-59953-330-8 (library edition : alk. paper) 1. New York Jets
(Football team)--History--Juvenile literature. I. Aikens, Jason. II. Title.

GV956.N37S74 2009
796.332'64097471--dc22

                                                2009011907

COVER PHOTO: The Jets celebrate a touchdown during a 2008 game.

Table of Contents

SPORTS WORDS & VOCABULARY WORDS: In this book, you will find many words that are new to you. You may also see familiar words used in new ways. The glossary on page 46 gives the meanings of football words, as well as "everyday" words that have special football meanings. These words appear in **bold type** throughout the book. The glossary on page 47 gives the meanings of vocabulary words that are not related to football. They appear in ***bold italic type*** throughout the book.

Meet the Jets

The sight of a football spiraling through the air is one of the most exciting images in sports. From the quarterback's fingertips to the receiver's hands, a lot of things must go right for a pass to be completed. Fans of the New York Jets know this better than anyone. The pass has been a big part of their team's history. That makes sense, especially considering that the Jets are named after a flying object.

When things go right for the Jets, they are tough to beat. During one magical season many *decades* ago, everything went perfectly—and the team changed the face of **professional** football. Since then, the New York players have tried to live up to that high standard.

This book tells the story of the Jets. They are a team with a great past, but they always look to the future. They understand what it takes to play winning football, and they never stop trying to achieve perfection on the field.

Leon Washington spikes the ball after a touchdown during a 2008 game. Teammates Jerricho Cotchery and Dustin Keller rush to join the celebration.

Way Back When

In 1958, New York City was the site of the most thrilling game in the history of the **National Football League (NFL)**. It took **overtime** to decide the **NFL Championship** that year between the Baltimore Colts and New York Giants. Afterward, the popularity of pro football skyrocketed. Two years later, the **American Football League (AFL)** began play.

The AFL believed there was room for two teams in New York. The new league placed a team called the Titans just across the river from the Giants. The Titans had some very good players, including receivers Don Maynard and Art Powell, and linebacker Larry Grantham. Their coach was Sammy Baugh, one of the greatest quarterbacks ever. The Titans played well, but they were in danger of going out of business by 1964.

In stepped Leon Hess and Sonny Werblin. They bought the team and changed its name to the Jets. They also hired Weeb Ewbank, the coach of the Colts from that famous 1958 game. In 1965, the Jets outbid the NFL for college quarterback Joe Namath.

By 1968, the Jets were the top team in the AFL. Namath broke many of the league's passing records. He combined with Maynard and a group of young stars to give New York a great offense. The team's defense, still led by Grantham, was also very good. New York won the **AFL Championship** and met Baltimore in **Super Bowl** III. The Jets shocked fans everywhere by beating the powerful Colts. The victory proved that the AFL was as good as the NFL. Two years later, the AFL and NFL *merged* into a single league.

Great things were expected of the Jets in the 1970s. New York had some terrific pass-catchers during this era, including Rich Caster, Jerome Barkum, Wesley Walker, and Mickey Shuler. But Namath suffered through one injury after another, and the team struggled.

By the early 1980s, a new group of players led the team that fans called "Gang Green." Joe Klecko, Mark Gastineau, Abdul Salaam, and Marty Lyons formed a great defensive line nicknamed the "New York **Sack** Exchange." Quarterback Richard Todd, running back Freeman McNeil, and Walker paced the offense. In the 1982 season, the Jets reached the title game of the **American Football Conference (AFC)** for the first time.

New York fans grew hungrier and hungrier for another Super Bowl victory. The Jets had terrific players—including quarterback Ken O'Brien and receiver Al Toon—but they always came up empty. In 1997, New York hired coach Bill Parcells to rebuild the team. He relied on four offensive stars—quarterback Vinny Testaverde, running back Curtis Martin, and receivers Keyshawn Johnson and Wayne Chrebet. The Jets made it back to the **AFC Championship** game in 1998. But just as in 1982, the team fell one win short of a return trip to the Super Bowl. New York fans would not be satisfied until the Jets won the big game again. As the 21st *century* neared, it was time to start a new run at the NFL Championship.

LEFT: Joe Klecko, Marty Lyons, Abdul Salaam, and Mark Gastineau—the "New York Sack Exchange"—pose on the floor of the New York Stock Exchange.　　**ABOVE**: Ken O'Brien, one of the top quarterbacks in team history.

The Team Today

The Jets have always been at their best when they build around a good quarterback. From 2002 to 2007, that player was Chad Pennington. The son of a football coach, he was a popular team leader and a very accurate passer. Like Joe Namath, Pennington had bad luck with injuries. But when he was healthy, New York had an excellent team. The Jets hoped to find another great quarterback when they **drafted** Mark Sanchez in 2009.

To help their passing game, the Jets have depended on powerful offensive linemen. Their leaders in recent years were Kevin Mawae, D'Brickashaw Ferguson, and Nick Mangold. The team also had several speedy runners and receivers, including Leon Washington, Thomas Jones, Laveranues Coles, and Jerricho Cotchery.

The Jets share the **AFC East** with the New England Patriots, a team that has built a football *dynasty*. Their games with the "Pats" are the highlight of each season. The Jets hope to build a dynasty of their own. By mixing older players with *emerging* stars, the team and its fans are excited to make a return to the Super Bowl.

Thomas Jones talks things over with Nick Mangold, D'Brickashaw Ferguson, and Brandon Moore during a 2008 game.

Home Turf

The Jets have called three stadiums home since 1960. They played their first four seasons in the Polo Grounds. It was an old-time baseball stadium. From 1964 to 1983, the team played in Shea Stadium, another baseball field. They shared it with the Mets.

In 1984, the Jets moved from New York to New Jersey. They host their games in Giants Stadium in the Meadowlands Sports Complex. They share the stadium with the Giants. Both teams continue to call themselves "New York."

When one team plays at home, the other is on the road—except when they square off against each other. The Jets and Giants have separate locker rooms. In 2007, work began on a new stadium located next door to Giants Stadium. The Jets will again share it with the Giants.

BY THE NUMBERS

- *There are 80,062 seats for football in the Jets' stadium.*
- *The stadium cost more than $1.4 billion to build.*
- *As of 2009, the Jets had retired three numbers: 12 (Joe Namath), 13 (Don Maynard), and 73 (Joe Klecko).*

The Jets line up for a play on offense during a 2008 game in their stadium.

Dressed for Success

In 1960, the New York Titans took the field in blue, gold, and white uniforms. The players wore these colors until 1964. That season new owner Leon Hess decided green and white would look better. Those were the same colors of his gasoline stations.

The Jets switched to a darker shade of green in 1990, but the team's basic colors remain the same. Like many NFL teams, the Jets sometimes wear their old colors for special games. In 2007, the blue and gold of the Titans made a return.

The biggest changes in New York's look have occurred on the

helmet. For many years, the Jets wore white helmets with green stripes and a green football that said *JETS*. In 1978, the team switched to green helmets and changed their **logo**. The new design showed a ***futuristic*** jet. In 1998, the Jets went back to a helmet that was closer to the original design.

Art Powell models the original uniform of the Titans.

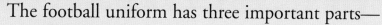

UNIFORM BASICS

The football uniform has three important parts—
- Helmet
- Jersey
- Pants

Helmets used to be made out of leather, and they did not have facemasks—ouch! Today, helmets are made of super-strong plastic. The uniform top, or jersey, is made of thick fabric. It fits snugly around a player so that tacklers cannot grab it and pull him down. The pants come down just over the knees.

There is a lot more to a football uniform than what you see on the outside. Air can be pumped inside the helmet to give it a snug, padded fit. The jersey covers shoulder pads, and sometimes a rib protector called a flak jacket. The pants include pads that protect the hips, thighs, *tailbone*, and knees.

Football teams have two sets of uniforms— one dark and one light. This makes it easier to tell two teams apart on the field. Almost all teams wear their dark uniforms at home and their light ones on the road.

Darrelle Revis wears the Jets' 2008 home uniform.

We Won!

The story of the 1968 Jets is one of the most famous in sports. For many years, the NFL and AFL had competed for the hearts of football fans across the country. In 1966, the leagues agreed to merge. The new league would still be called the NFL.

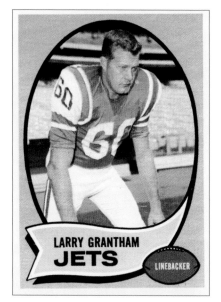

LARRY GRANTHAM
JETS
LINEBACKER

Many experts thought this was a bad idea. They believed that NFL teams would destroy the AFL newcomers. If that happened, fans would lose interest in pro football.

In the first two Super Bowls, the Green Bay Packers defeated their AFL opponents with ease. As Super Bowl III drew near, the situation looked like it would get worse. The Baltimore Colts had a great team. They beat the Cleveland Browns in the NFL Championship, 34–0. The Browns were an excellent team. What chance could the AFL champions possibly have?

Joe Namath thought they had a very good chance. He was the quarterback of the Jets, and his team had risen to the top of the AFL in 1968 with a record of 11–3. Namath had three excellent receivers in Don Maynard, George Sauer, and Pete Lammons. He also had

good blockers to protect him, including Winston Hill, Dave Herman, and Randy Rasmussen. New York's offensive line opened big holes for running backs Matt Snell and Emerson Boozer. As head coach Weeb Ewbank knew, teamwork was the key to the team's great offense.

New York's defense was pretty good, too. Larry Grantham led a solid group that included Johnny Sample, Al Atkinson, Ralph Baker,

LEFT: Larry Grantham, the Jets' leader on defense.
ABOVE: Don Maynard catches a touchdown pass against the Oakland Raiders in 1968.

17

Randy Beverly, and John Dockery. Sample had once been traded away by the Colts. Super Bowl III was a chance for him to get some revenge.

The Jets earned the right to play the Colts after beating the Oakland Raiders in the AFL Championship. The Raiders led late in the fourth quarter, but Namath stunned them with a 52-yard bomb to Maynard to get within striking distance of the end zone. Moments later they connected again for the winning touchdown. New York won 27–23.

In the days before Super Bowl III, the Colts were confident, and the Jets were quiet. Namath decided to shake things up. He predicted that New York would win. In fact, he guaranteed it!

Namath's prediction angered the Colts, but it gave the Jets confidence. Led by their fearless quarterback, they played a great first half. The Jets went into the locker room with a 7–0 lead.

The Colts were in shock. Their confusion continued in the second half. Namath barely threw the ball. Instead, he handed off to Snell, who kept picking up big yardage. New York ate up lots of time, and Jim Turner kicked three **field goals** to make the score 16–0. The Colts scored a touchdown in the fourth quarter, but it was too little, too late. The final score was 16–7.

As Namath ran off the field, he held up his right index finger to show the world which team was number one. The real winner was pro football. No one would ever again doubt the decision to merge the AFL and NFL.

LEFT: Joe Namath hands off to Matt Snell during Super Bowl III.
ABOVE: Namath shows football fans who's #1 after New York's victory.

Go-To Guys

To be a true star in the NFL, you need more than fast feet and a big body. You have to be a "go-to guy"—someone the coach wants on the field at the end of a big game. Fans of the Titans and Jets have had a lot to cheer about over the years, including these great stars …

THE PIONEERS

DON MAYNARD   Receiver

- BORN: 1/25/1935   • PLAYED FOR TEAM: 1960 TO 1972

Don Maynard was the first player signed by the Titans. The former college track star caught 72 passes in his first season with the team. By the time he retired, he had caught more passes for more yards than anyone in football history.

LARRY GRANTHAM   Linebacker

- BORN: 9/16/1938   • PLAYED FOR TEAM: 1960 TO 1972

During the 1960s, the Jets relied as much on their defense as they did on their offense. The heart of that unit was Larry Grantham. He played all 10 years that the AFL was in existence and was an **All-Star** five times.

ABOVE: Don Maynard
RIGHT: Pat Leahy watches a kick sail between the goal posts.

JOE NAMATH   Quarterback

- BORN: 5/31/1943   • PLAYED FOR TEAM: 1965 TO 1976

Thanks to Joe Namath, football fans accepted the AFL as the equal of the NFL. He was the best passer in either league before knee injuries slowed him down. Namath was the **Most Valuable Player (MVP)** in Super Bowl III and the first pro quarterback to throw for more than 4,000 yards in a season.

PAT LEAHY   Kicker

- BORN: 3/19/1951   • PLAYED FOR TEAM: 1974 TO 1991

Pat Leahy led his college team to three national soccer championships. Jets fans know him as the club's all-time scoring leader. Leahy kicked 304 field goals and 558 extra points for a total of 1,470 points.

JOE KLECKO   Defensive Lineman

- BORN: 10/15/1953   • PLAYED FOR TEAM: 1977 TO 1987

No one wanted to mess with Joe Klecko. He was a national boxing champion twice in college and one of the strongest tacklers in the NFL. Klecko was respected by opponents and loved by the fans. His number was just the third retired by the Jets.

WESLEY WALKER   Receiver

- BORN: 5/26/1955   • PLAYED FOR TEAM: 1977 TO 1989

Wesley Walker could barely see out of one eye. It hardly made a difference, because once the ball was snapped, no one could outrun him. Walker made catches of 20 and 30 yards almost every week. In 1986, he caught four touchdowns in a game.

MODERN STARS

MARK GASTINEAU — Defensive Lineman

- BORN: 11/20/1956 • PLAYED FOR TEAM: 1979 TO 1988

During the 1980s, the king of the quarterback sack was Mark Gastineau. He was almost impossible to block one-on-one. Gastineau was Defensive Player of the Year in 1982. Three years later, he set a record with 22 sacks.

FREEMAN McNEIL — Running Back

- BORN: 4/22/1959
- PLAYED FOR TEAM: 1981 TO 1992

Few players in NFL history have been as hard to tackle as Freeman McNeil. He had size, speed, and great moves. McNeil led the NFL in rushing in 1982. Along with teammate Johnny Hector, he gave the Jets a great **backfield**.

MO LEWIS — Linebacker

- BORN: 10/21/1969
- PLAYED FOR TEAM: 1991 TO 2003

Mo Lewis was the team's defensive captain for seven seasons. He was a *ferocious* tackler and a great leader. Lewis continued New York's *tradition* of outstanding linebackers, which included Greg Buttle, Lance Mehl, Kyle Clifton, and Marvin Jones.

WAYNE CHREBET — Receiver

- BORN: 8/14/1973   • PLAYED FOR TEAM: 1995 TO 2005

After graduating from college, Wayne Chrebet was not drafted by a single NFL team. He asked for a tryout with the Jets and soon became their top receiver. Chrebet was at his best on third down when the team needed him the most.

CURTIS MARTIN — Running Back

- BORN: 5/1/1973   • PLAYED FOR TEAM: 1998 TO 2005

Curtis Martin gave the Jets a great running attack. He gained 1,000 yards in each of his first seven seasons with the team and missed only one game. Martin was the NFL rushing champion in 2004 at the age of 31.

D'BRICKASHAW FERGUSON — Offensive Lineman

- BORN: 12/10/1983
- FIRST SEASON WITH TEAM: 2006

Good blocking is vital to a successful offense. In 2006, the Jets rebuilt their offensive line around D'Brickashaw Ferguson. He was big, quick, and light on his feet. He also held a black belt in karate and a brown belt in taekwondo—which made him an even better blocker!

LEFT: Mark Gastineau
RIGHT: D'Brickashaw Ferguson

On the Sidelines

For a team with just one championship, the Jets have had a *remarkable* number of fine coaches. Their first, Sammy Baugh, had been a superstar quarterback in the 1930s and 1940s. He led a rag-tag group of players to seven wins in each of their first two seasons. Another **Hall of Famer**, Bulldog Turner, coached the team in 1962.

Weeb Ewbank followed Turner. Ewbank had taken a young, disorganized team in Baltimore and turned it into a champion. He did the same with the Jets. Players loved Ewbank. He knew how to get the most out of them.

The Jets came within one victory of returning to the Super Bowl in the 1982 and 1998 seasons. Their coach that first time was Walt Michaels. He had played for Ewbank in the 1950s and was his assistant with the Jets in the 1960s. Bill Parcells was on the sidelines in 1998. He believed that a coach should get to decide which players belong on the **roster**, instead of other *executives* with the team. The Jets gave him the green light, and he turned them into winners.

Weeb Ewbank watches the action from the sideline during Super Bowl III. He coached the Jets to an upset victory over the Baltimore Colts.

One Great Day

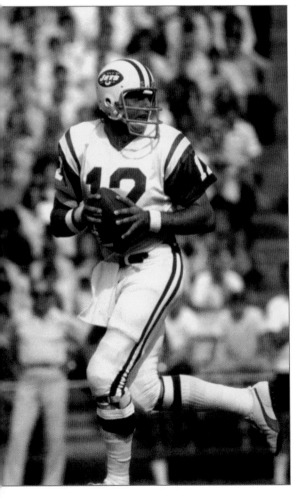

Growing up in Beaver Falls, Pennsylvania, Joe Namath *idolized* Johnny Unitas. Namath loved the way Unitas could *dominate* a game with his strong arm and sharp mind. It was no coincidence that Namath ended up being the same kind of quarterback. Of course, that was about all they had in common. Unitas sported a flat-top crewcut, dressed plainly, and kept his thoughts to himself. Namath had long hair, wore wild clothes, and dated movie stars.

When Namath and Unitas met on the field, however, it was all about throwing the football. In the second week of the 1972 season, the Jets traveled to Baltimore to face the Colts. Unitas was in his final year with the team. Namath had missed most of the

1971 season with an injury. Fans of both teams were hoping for the best, but many were expecting the worst.

What they saw was the most unbelievable showcase of passing in NFL history. Namath and Unitas were in top form. They drilled pass after pass to their receivers, marching their teams up and down the field. The Colts played a **zone defense** in the first half, and Namath picked it apart. They played man-on-man in the second half, and Namath was even better.

RICHARD CASTER • WR

The Jets held a slim lead in the fourth quarter when Namath saw Rich Caster running in the clear. Namath lofted a long pass into his hands for a 79-yard touchdown. The next time New York had the ball, Caster faked the same play and then quickly changed directions. He was open again, and Namath hit him with an 80-yard scoring pass!

The Jets didn't have much better luck with Unitas. The 39-year-old legend rolled up 376 yards and three touchdowns. Namath finished with 496 yards and six touchdowns. The Jets won 44–34.

LEFT: Joe Namath drops back to pass during his amazing game against the Baltimore Colts.
ABOVE: Rich Caster, Namath's favorite target on that day.

Legend Has It

Which Jet was nicknamed the Green Lantern?

LEGEND HAS IT that Wayne Chrebet was. Chrebet teamed with Keyshawn Johnson to give the Jets two good receivers in the mid-1990s. After Johnson joined the Tampa Bay Buccaneers, he was asked to compare himself with Chrebet. Johnson said that he was a star in the sky. Chrebet, he joked, was more like a flashlight. The first time the two teams played, Chrebet scored the game-winning touchdown. After that, everyone called him the Green Lantern after a famous comic book superhero.

ABOVE: Wayne Chrebet

Who was the best dancer on the Jets?

LEGEND HAS IT that Mark Gastineau was. Gastineau was one of the best pass rushers in the NFL. Nothing gave him a bigger thrill than tackling the quarterback behind the **line of scrimmage**. After taking down an opposing passer, Gastineau would break into a wild "sack dance." Jets fans loved it, but the league had a different opinion. After the 1983 season—when Gastineau had 19 sacks and did his dance 19 times—the NFL passed a rule against "unsportsmanlike taunting." From that point on, Gastineau's dancing days were over.

What was the Jets' most famous defeat?

LEGEND HAS IT that the "Heidi Game" was. In November of 1968, the Jets played the Raiders in Oakland, California. New York fans tuned in by the millions—these were the two best teams in the league. Because the game was played on the West Coast, it was late on the East Coast by the time the fourth quarter began. The Jets were leading 32–29 with just over a minute left when suddenly the game blinked off the air. It was replaced by the TV movie *Heidi*, which was scheduled to start on NBC at 7:00 P.M. sharp. Jets fans were ***outraged***—especially when the Raiders scored 14 points to win 43–32. Angry fans phoned NBC to complain. The network quickly realized just how popular AFL football had become!

It Really Happened

For football's most passionate fans, *Monday Night Football* is the perfect end to a fun weekend of games. The show became an American tradition in the 1970s and remains one today. Every Monday during the NFL season, millions of people from all over the country stay up late into the night to see how the game turns out.

That wasn't the case when the Jets met the Miami Dolphins on October 23rd, 2000. After three quarters, Miami was ahead 30–7. "This game is over," one of the Jets' own announcers said.

He spoke too soon. The Jets came alive and caught the Dolphins by surprise. Vinny Testaverde threw long touchdown passes to Laveranues Coles and Wayne Chrebet. The Jets scored another touchdown on a short pass, and John Hall booted a field goal. New York tied the score 30–30!

LEFT: Jumbo Elliott holds on to the game-tying touchdown pass against the Miami Dolphins.
RIGHT: John Hall and Tom Tupa celebrate the game-winning field goal.

The Dolphins regained their composure and took a 37–30 lead. But in the final moments, the Jets scored again on a trick play. Jumbo Elliott, an offensive lineman, batted, bobbled, and finally caught a three-yard pass in the end zone to send the game into overtime. Hall kicked a field goal a few minutes later to give the Jets a 40–37 victory.

New York's **comeback** was the greatest in the history of *Monday Night Football*—and the second-greatest ever in a regular-season game. In the amazing fourth quarter, the Jets made 20 first downs, as opposed to just one for the Dolphins. Of New York's four touchdowns in the final period, three were scored by players who had never reached the end zone before. To this day, Jets fans call the game the "Midnight Miracle."

Team Spirit

The New Jersey Meadowlands are transformed into a sea of green when the Jets play their home games. Hours before kick-off, fans begin arriving in the stadium parking lot to tailgate and swap stories about the highs and lows of the team's past. Once in the stadium, Jets fans are loud, proud, and wildly enthusiastic. As the game goes on, chants of "J-E-T-S! Jets! Jets! Jets!" get louder and louder—especially when the team is ahead.

Between games, Jets fans are among the most generous in the league. They often team up with players to donate time and money to good causes. It is a great chance to help others while standing shoulder-to-shoulder with their heroes.

In a region with more than 20 million people, there are always those in need. The Jets Foundation not only works with local charities, it has many programs of its own. One of the most popular is "Generation Jets Academy: Be Lean & Green," which battles childhood obesity.

Ed Anzalone—who is known as "Fireman Ed"—is one of the team's most famous fans. He usually leads the "J-E-T-S! Jets! Jets! Jets!" chant.

Timeline

In this timeline, each Super Bowl is listed under the year it was played. Remember that the Super Bowl is held early in the year and is actually part of the previous season. For example, Super Bowl XLIII was played on February 1st, 2009, but it was the championship of the 2008 NFL season.

1965
Don Maynard ties for the league lead in touchdowns.

1969
The Jets win Super Bowl III.

1960
The team plays its first season as the Titans.

1967
Joe Namath passes for 4,000 yards.

1978
Wesley Walker leads the NFL in receiving yards.

A button from the team's early years.

Joe Namath

Freeman
McNeil

Curtis
Martin

1982
Freeman McNeil is
the NFL's top rusher.

2002
Chad Pennington is
the NFL's top-rated
quarterback.

2004
Curtis Martin leads
the NFL with 1,697
rushing yards.

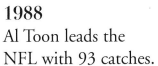

1988
Al Toon leads the
NFL with 93 catches.

1998
Vinny Testaverde leads
the Jets to a 12–4 record.

2009
The Jets draft
Mark Sanchez.

Al
Toon

Fun Facts

RISE AND WALK

Dennis Byrd was a rising star with the Jets when he injured his neck during a 1992 game. Doctors said he might never walk again. Byrd made a miraculous recovery. Today he gives speeches to inspire other injury victims.

A LITTLE ENGLISH

In 1972, Bobby Howfield led the AFC in scoring with 121 points. The 5′ 8″ kicker was an English soccer star who never played a down of football before coming to the NFL. Howfield once scored four goals in an English soccer game.

LET IT ROLL

In 1969, punter Steve O'Neill punted a ball from his own end zone against the Denver Broncos. The ball soared more than 70 yards in the air and rolled all the way to the other end of the field. It stopped just short of the goal line for a record 98-yard punt!

BY GEORGE!

New York's leading receiver in Super Bowl III was George Sauer. He caught eight passes for 133 yards. Sauer was an **All-Pro** two times in the AFL. Sauer's father was even more famous. George Sauer Sr. was an **All-American** in college during the 1930s and is a member of the College Football Hall of Fame.

George **SAUER**
NEW YORK JETS • END

TANKS A LOT

One of Joe Namath's best blockers in the 1960s was 340-pound Sherman Plunkett. Teammates nicknamed him "Tank" after the Sherman tanks of World War II.

RATINGS CHAMP

In 1986, Ken O'Brien passed for 431 yards and four touchdowns against the Seattle Seahawks. His **quarterback rating** was a "perfect" 158.3—the highest possible score for an NFL quarterback. Earlier that season, he threw for 479 yards against the Miami Dolphins.

LEFT: Dennis Byrd   **ABOVE**: George Sauer

Talking Football

"When you win, nothing hurts."

—Joe Namath, on why he continued to play on aching knees

"Being a quarterback in New York isn't easy."

—Richard Todd, on trying to follow in Joe Namath's footsteps

"He's a wild man on the field—he plays because he loves the game."

—Marvin Jones, on fellow linebacker Mo Lewis

"I wanted to be a professional football player and a New York Jet."

—Freeman McNeil, on why he played so hard through good times and bad

"I played the best, I believe I passed the test. I'm glad this is over, because I need the rest!"

—Don Maynard, at his Hall of Fame ceremony in 1987

"It's very rewarding to realize that at one time, we were the best defensive line in the NFL."

—*Marty Lyons, on the "New York Sack Exchange"*

"In the NFL, everyone's good. You have to study more and be a student of the game."

—*Darrelle Revis, on what it takes to be successful in the NFL*

"The best times of my life were the days that I played ball. You could be a child and have fun and still get paid for it."

—*Greg Buttle, on why he loved playing linebacker for the Jets*

"He inspired me every day. I loved the way he played and how he never backed down from anything. He was an incredible teammate. He was a warrior."

—*Curtis Martin, on Wayne Chrebet*

LEFT: Richard Todd   **ABOVE**: Marty Lyons

39

For the Record

The great Jets teams and players have left their marks on the record books. These are the "best of the best" …

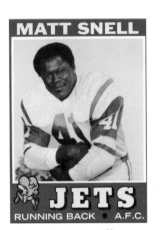

MATT SNELL

JETS
RUNNING BACK • A.F.C.

Matt Snell

JETS AWARD WINNERS

WINNER	AWARD	YEAR
Matt Snell	AFL Rookie of the Year*	1964
Joe Namath	AFL Rookie of the Year	1965
Joe Namath	AFL All-Star Game co-MVP	1966
Verlon Biggs	AFL All-Star Game co-MVP	1967
Don Maynard	AFL All-Star Game co-MVP	1968
Joe Namath	AFL All-Star Game co-MVP	1968
Joe Namath	AFL Most Valuable Player	1968
Joe Namath	Super Bowl III MVP	1968
Joe Namath	Comeback Player of the Year	1974
Erik McMillan	Defensive Rookie of the Year	1988
Hugh Douglas	Defensive Rookie of the Year	1995
Jonathan Vilma	Defensive Rookie of the Year	2004
Chad Pennington	Comeback Player of the Year	2006

The Rookie of the Year award is given to the league's best first-year player.

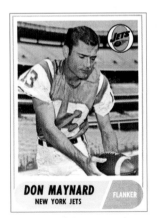

DON MAYNARD
NEW YORK JETS   FLANKER

Don Maynard

Joe
Namath

JETS

JOE NAMATH • QB

JETS ACHIEVEMENTS

ACHIEVEMENT	YEAR
AFL East Champions	1968
AFL Champions	1968
Super Bowl III Champions	1968*
AFL East Champions	1969
AFC East Champions	1998
AFC East Champions	2002

Super Bowls are played early the following year, but the game is counted as the championship of this season.

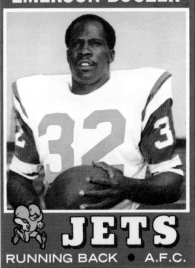

EMERSON BOOZER

JETS

RUNNING BACK • A.F.C.

Jim TURNER
NEW YORK JETS • KICKER

ABOVE: Emerson Boozer and Jim Turner, heroes for the 1968 champs.
LEFT: Chad Pennington, the 2006 Comeback Player of the Year.

Pinpoints

The history of a football team is made up of many smaller stories. These stories take place all over the map—not just in the city a team calls "home." Match the pushpins on these maps to the Team Facts and you will begin to see the story of the Jets unfold!

TEAM FACTS

1 East Rutherford, New Jersey—*The Jets have played here since 1984.*

2 Beaver Falls, Pennsylvania—*Joe Namath was born here.*

3 Cincinnati, Ohio—*Abdul Salaam was born here.*

4 Richmond, Indiana—*Weeb Ewbank was born here.*

5 Knoxville, Tennessee—*Chad Pennington was born here.*

6 Jacksonville, Florida—*Laveranues Coles was born here.*

7 Jackson, Mississippi—*Freeman McNeil was born here.*

8 Mobile, Alabama—*Rich Caster was born here.*

9 Oklahoma City, Oklahoma—*Sherman Plunkett was born here.*

10 St. Paul, Nebraska—*Randy Rasmussen was born here.*

11 Los Angeles, California—*Keyshawn Johnson was born here.*

12 Bushey, England—*Bobby Howfield was born here.*

Abdul Salaam

Play Ball

Football is a sport played by two teams on a field that is 100 yards long. The game is divided into four 15-minute quarters. Each team must have 11 players on the field at all times. The group that has the ball is called the offense. The group trying to keep the offense from moving the ball forward is called the defense.

A football game is made up of a series of "plays." Each play starts and ends with a referee's signal. A play begins when the center snaps the ball between his legs to the quarterback. The quarterback then gives the ball to a teammate, throws (or "passes") the ball to a teammate, or runs with the ball himself. The job of the defense is to tackle the player with the ball or stop the quarterback's pass. A play ends when the ball (or player holding the ball) is "down." The offense must move the ball forward at least 10 yards every four downs. If it fails to do so, the other team is given the ball. If the offense has not made 10 yards after three downs—and does not want to risk losing the ball—it can kick (or "punt") the ball to make the other team start from its own end of the field.

At each end of a football field is a goal line, which divides the field from the end zone. A team must run or pass the ball over the goal line to score a touchdown, which counts for six points. After scoring a touchdown, a team can try a short kick for one "extra point," or try again to run or pass across the goal line for two points. Teams can score three points from anywhere on the field by kicking the ball between the goal posts. This is called a field goal.

The defense can score two points if it tackles a player while he is in his own end zone. This is called a safety. The defense can also score points by taking the ball away from the offense and crossing the opposite goal line for a touchdown. The team with the most points after 60 minutes is the winner.

Football may seem like a very hard game to understand, but the more you play and watch football, the more "little things" you are likely to notice. The next time you are at a game, look for these plays:

PLAY LIST

BLITZ—A play in which the defense sends extra tacklers after the quarterback. If the quarterback sees a blitz coming, he passes the ball quickly. If he does not, he can end up at the bottom of a very big pile!

DRAW—A play in which the offense pretends it will pass the ball, and then gives it to a running back. If the offense can "draw" the defense to the quarterback and his receivers, the running back should have lots of room to run.

FLY PATTERN—A play in which a team's fastest receiver is told to "fly" past the defensive backs for a long pass. Many long touchdowns are scored on this play.

SQUIB KICK—A play in which the ball is kicked a short distance on purpose. A squib kick is used when the team kicking off does not want the other team's fastest player to catch the ball and run with it.

SWEEP—A play in which the ball carrier follows a group of teammates moving sideways to "sweep" the defense out of the way. A good sweep gives the runner a chance to gain a lot of yards before he is tackled or forced out of bounds.

Glossary

FOOTBALL WORDS TO KNOW

AFC CHAMPIONSHIP—The game played to determine which AFC team will go to the Super Bowl.

AFC EAST—A division for teams that play in the eastern part of the country.

AFL CHAMPIONSHIP—The game that decided the winner of the American Football League.

ALL-AMERICAN—A college player voted as the best at his position.

ALL-PRO—An honor given to the best players at their position at the end of each season.

ALL-STAR—A player picked to play in the AFL All-Star Game of the 1960s.

AMERICAN FOOTBALL CONFERENCE (AFC)—One of two groups of teams that make up the NFL. The winner of the AFC plays the winner of the National Football Conference (NFC) in the Super Bowl.

AMERICAN FOOTBALL LEAGUE (AFL)—The football league that began play in 1960 and later merged with the NFL.

BACKFIELD—The players who line up in back of the line of scrimmage. On offense, the quarterback and running backs are in the backfield.

DRAFTED—Chosen from a group of the best college players. The NFL draft is held each spring.

FIELD GOALS—Goals from the field, kicked over the crossbar and between the goal posts. A field goal is worth three points.

HALL OF FAMER—A player who has been honored as being among the greatest ever and is enshrined in the College or Pro Football Hall of Fame.

LINE OF SCRIMMAGE—The imaginary line that separates the offense and defense before each play begins.

MOST VALUABLE PLAYER (MVP)—The award given each year to the league's best player; also given to the best player in the Super Bowl and Pro Bowl.

NATIONAL FOOTBALL LEAGUE (NFL)—The league that started in 1920 and is still operating today.

NFL CHAMPIONSHIP—The game played to decide the winner of the league each year from 1933 to 1969.

OVERTIME—The extra period played when a game is tied after 60 minutes.

PROFESSIONAL—A player or team that plays a sport for money.

QUARTERBACK RATING—A special statistic that measures how well a quarterback has played.

ROSTER—The list of a team's active players.

SACK—A tackle of the quarterback behind the line of scrimmage.

SUPER BOWL—The championship of football, played between the winners of the NFC and AFC.

ZONE DEFENSE—A defense in which players are responsible for guarding an area of the field rather than covering a specific offensive player.

OTHER WORDS TO KNOW

CENTURY—A period of 100 years.

COMEBACK—The process of catching up from behind, or making up a large deficit.

DECADES—Periods of 10 years; also specific periods, such as the 1950s.

DOMINATE—Completely control.

DYNASTY—A family, group, or team that maintains power over time.

EMERGING—Becoming more important.

EXECUTIVES—People who help run a business.

FEROCIOUS—Extremely intense.

FUTURISTIC—Having or involving modern technology or design.

IDOLIZED—Admired greatly.

LOGO—A symbol or design that represents a company or team.

MERGED—Joined forces.

OUTRAGED—Extremely upset.

REMARKABLE—Unusual or exceptional.

TAILBONE—The bone that protects the base of the spine.

TRADITION—A belief or custom that is handed down from generation to generation.

Places to Go

ON THE ROAD

NEW YORK JETS
50 State Route 120
East Rutherford, New Jersey 07073
(800) 469-5387

THE PRO FOOTBALL HALL OF FAME
2121 George Halas Drive NW
Canton, Ohio 44708
(330) 456-8207

ON THE WEB

THE NATIONAL FOOTBALL LEAGUE   www.nfl.com
  • *Learn more about the National Football League*

THE NEW YORK JETS   www.newyorkjets.com
  • *Learn more about the Jets*

THE PRO FOOTBALL HALL OF FAME   www.profootballhof.com
  • *Learn more about football's greatest players*

ON THE BOOKSHELF

To learn more about the sport of football, look for these books at your library or bookstore:

  • Stewart, Mark and Kennedy, Mike. *Touchdown: the Power and Precision of Football's Perfect Play*. Minneapolis, Minnesota: Millbrook Press, 2009.

  • Buckley Jr., James. *The Child's World Encyclopedia of the NFL*. Mankato, Minnesota: Child's World, 2008.

  • Gigliotti, Jim. *Football*. Ann Arbor, Michigan: Cherry Lake Publishing, 2009.

  • Jacobs, Greg. *The Everything Kids' Football Book: the all-time greats, legendary teams, today's superstars—and tips on playing like a pro*. Cincinnati, Ohio: Adams Media, 2008.

47

Index

PAGE NUMBERS IN **BOLD** REFER TO ILLUSTRATIONS.

The Team

MARK STEWART has written more than 50 books on football, and over 200 sports books for kids. He grew up in New York City during the 1960s rooting for the Giants and Jets, and now takes his two daughters, Mariah and Rachel, to watch them play in their home state of New Jersey. Mark comes from a family of

writers. His grandfather was Sunday Editor of *The New York Times* and his mother was Articles Editor of *The Ladies' Home Journal* and *McCall's*. Mark has profiled hundreds of athletes over the last 20 years. He has also written several books about New York and New Jersey. Mark is a graduate of Duke University, with a degree in History. He lives with his daughters and wife Sarah overlooking Sandy Hook, New Jersey.

JASON AIKENS is the Collections Curator at the Pro Football Hall of Fame. He is responsible for the preservation of the Pro Football Hall of Fame's collection of artifacts and memorabilia and obtaining new donations of memorabilia from current players and NFL teams. Jason has a Bachelor of Arts in History from Michigan State University and a Master's in History from Western Michigan University where he concentrated on sports history. Jason has been working for the Pro Football Hall of Fame since 1997; before that he was an intern at the College Football Hall of Fame. Jason's family has roots in California and has been following the St. Louis Rams since their

days in Los Angeles, California. He lives with his wife Cynthia and their daughter Angelina in Canton, Ohio.